1. Introduction

1.1 Purpose of this Handbook

This Handbook aims to help law enforcement professionals to understand the ethical issues and challenges inherent in the use of Artificial Intelligence (AI) systems and associated AI technologies in the context of law enforcement. The Handbook is for use at a strategic level, during the planning, procurement and operational phases. It can act as a reference point for the ethical assessment of AI systems, technologies and tools and in specific scenarios such as domestic law enforcement and counter-terrorism. This handbook may also be used for the training of people using AI systems, technologies and tools and for raising awareness and making possible the translation of the ethical and legal framework to an operational and practical guideline. This handbook has received funding from the European Union's Horizon 2020 research and innovation programme under Grant Agreement No.786629, Project MAGNETO.

The EU regulates emerging AI technologies for law enforcement through the adoption of legal instruments that are relevant and applicable both at the R&D stage and at the deployment phase. Privacy and data protection norms, fundamental rights provisions, EU safety standards, dual use and export control rules, as well as other specific legal instruments apply depending on the specific context in which a technology may be employed. The EU approach also entails the promotion of societal acceptance of new AI technologies by enforcing, among other things, the principles of "privacy by design" and "privacy by default" [Ref1].

The main legal documents for the implementation and deployment of AI technologies in law enforcement are the General Data Protection Regulation 2016/679/EU (hereafter GDPR) [Ref2], the Directive 2016/680 on the protection of natural persons with regard to the processing of personal data by competent authorities for the purposes of the prevention, investigation, detection or prosecution of criminal offences or the execution of criminal penalties (DPLED) [Ref3], as well as the Recommendation in regard to automatic processing in the context of profiling, which provides a policy framework to be implemented by the members of the CoE [Ref4].

In this context, the general ethical framework of this handbook complements the legal requirements and is based primarily on international institutions' directives such as the European Convention of Human Rights (ECHR) and the Charter of Fundamental Rights of the European Union [Ref5]. The specific ethical values and principles underlying the framework for the ethical impact assessment process developed in this handbook are derived from the Ethics Guidelines for Trustworthy AI document published by the European Commission's High-Level Expert Group on Artificial Intelligence (HLEG) [Ref6].

The key parts of the Handbook commence in Section 4 after Section 1 Introduction, Section 2 Contents and Section 3 the Glossary. It is structured as follows:

- Section 4 outlines the key points of applied ethics and defines what constitutes an ethical concern. It provides the background to ethics in the context of the use or misuse of AI systems for law enforcement and useful reference documents. It also presents the main ethical issues of AI technologies in the context of the ethics of surveillance, underlying the four major categories:
    - Public space surveillance: smart CCTV;
    - Network & targeted device surveillance (cyber-surveillance): Deep packet inspection for Internet surveillance, content surveillance on targeted devices, location tracking;
    - Biometrics: face recognition;
    - Data matching, linkage & analysis: including big data, data mining, and visualization of results).
- Section 5 proposes a framework for the ethical impact assessment of AI systems in law enforcement and the associated AI surveillance technologies. The Framework is supplemented by Ethical Risk Assessment (ERA) forms (Appendix 1), and Misuse Risk Assessment (MRA) forms (Appendix 2). These should be used in close association with this Handbook (in particular Section 4), which provides the background information needed for a thorough assessment.

1.2 Acknowledgements

The Handbook was created by Irina Marsh (formerly Stănciugelu), Nigel Hale and Dominic Kelly of CBRNE Ltd (www.cbrneltd.com).

The underlying research work was carried out within Project MAGNETO – Multimedia Analysis and Correlation Engine for Organised Crime Prevention and Investigation [Ref7]. MAGNETO is funded by the H2020 Programme of the European Union.

1.3 Contacts

If you have any queries or comments regarding the content of this Handbook, please contact Dominic Kelly, Managing Director CBRNE Ltd, via https://www.cbrneltd.com/contact_us.html

2. Contents

3. Abbreviations

Abbreviation	Meaning
AI	Artificial Intelligence
ALARP	As Low As Reasonably Practicable
APIS	Advanced Passenger Information System
apud	Latin 'in the writing of'. Used to cite a reference at second hand
CCTV	Closed Circuit Television)
CoE	Council of Europe
DPI	Deep Packet Inspection
DPIA	Data Protection Impact Assessment
DPLED	Directive 2016/680 of the European Union
EIA	Ethical Impact Assessment
EC	European Community
ECHR	European Convention of Human Rights
EIA	Ethical Impact Assessment
ER	Ethical Risk
ERA	Ethical Risk Assessment
ERCS	Ethical Risk Classification System
EU	European Union
LEA	Law Enforcement Agency
FTC	Federal Trade Commission
GDPR	General Data Protection Regulations
GSM	Global System for Mobile Communication
HLEG	High-Level Expert Group on Artificial Intelligence
ibidem	Latin 'in the same place'. Used to cite the immediately preceding reference
ICCPR	International Covenant on Civil and Political Rights
ISP	Internet Service Provider
IT	Internet Technologies
MRA	Misuse Risk Assessment
OECD	Organisation for Economic co-operation and development
PIA	Privacy Impact Assessment
PNR	Passenger Name Records
R&D	Research and Development
URL	Uniform Resource Locator

4. Ethical framework

The section outlines the key points of applied ethics and defines what constitutes an ethical problem. It describes the main ethical issues that the AI systems, technologies and tools pose in the context of the ethics of surveillance.

This section provides the context for the rest of the Handbook.

4.1 Introduction to applied ethics

Ethics is the systematic reflection on what is moral: where 'morality' is defined as the totality of opinions, decisions and actions with which people express what they consider is good or right [Ref 8].

Applied ethics is concerned with questions of what is right and wrong, good and bad, just and unjust in a specific social domain. Examples are bioethics, environmental ethics, healthcare ethics, ethics and war, and ethics and technology. Professional ethics is a form of applied ethics that is concerned with specialists – such as doctors, nurses and lawyers – as opposed to their field of study [Ref9]. Applied ethics involves deliberating over specific situations. According to Beauchamp, 'principles must be made specific for the context; otherwise moral guidelines will be empty and ineffectual' [Ref10]. Beauchamp proposes four moral principles as first principles and conditions of more specific moral conceptions: (1) respect for autonomy (the obligation to respect the decision making capacities of autonomous persons); 2) non-maleficence (the obligation to avoid causing harm); (3) beneficence (obligations to provide benefits and to balance benefits against risks), and (4) justice (obligations of fairness in the distribution of benefits and risks). To deliberate over specific situations often leads to a conflict of moral values. For example, healthcare professionals have a duty to care for all individuals, whereas law enforcement professionals are arguably more likely to compromise the status of one individual in order to safeguard society as a whole. In this sense, professional ethics considerations are more oriented towards the well-being of others, although the interpretation and scope of well-being may differ between professional domains [Ref11].

The perspective from which an individual considers a situation is likely to determine what constitutes an ethical problem. For example, law enforcement professionals who implement a policy may not face the same problems as those who draft the policy. Policymakers and managers are responsible for maximising the effectiveness of their resources; whereas frontline personnel are responsible for maximising the effectiveness of every action they take.

An ethical problem can be characterised as follows [Ref12]:

- The problem cannot be thoroughly described before it arises; there is a general frame that contain the ethical problem and, through consideration, is adjusted in the details
- The problem unfolds concurrently with the decision-making process
- The problem does not have a single best solution, and
- There are many possible alternatives for action.

4.1.1 The relationship between law and ethics

In democratic countries, legislation represents the ethical position of a majority of society at a particular point in time. As such, it is closely related to ethics, but the two remain distinct. Law or a legal system is distinguished from morality or a moral system by having explicit written rules and penalties, with officials who interpret the laws and apply penalties. Although there is often considerable overlap in conduct governed by morality and that governed by law, laws are often evaluated on moral grounds. Moral criticism is often used to support a change in the law. Some maintained that the interpretation of law must make use of morality [Ref13].

Ethics also provides a means through which to determine which legislation to apply in a given situation. There is always scope to reflect on the extent to which different laws apply; in fact, judges are empowered to interpret the law to allow trade-offs that are appropriate for specific circumstances.

Law may be considered a tool for ethical decision-making. While it creates some questions – such as which law to apply in a given situation – it provides guidance on what is considered 'right' by society at a given point in time.

4.2 AI systems in the context of ethics of surveillance

Surveillance may be defined as "the keeping of watch over someone or something. Technological surveillance is the use of techniques or devices to detect attributes, activities, people, trends, or events" [Ref14].

We identify 6 features of contemporary technological surveillance [Ref15]:

- is driven by the desire to bring systems together, leading to an increased convergence of formerly discrete surveillance systems and an exponential increase in surveillance capacity;
- is increasingly growing and spreading by expanding its uses for the purposes of control, governance, security, profit and entertainment, and with the help of new and intensified technological capabilities, particularly the rise of computerised databases;
- has a levelling effect on hierarchies of surveillance, due to new target populations being monitored with new and intensified technological possibilities;
- works across state as well as non-state institutions;
- is primarily directed towards human bodies that are understood as a hybrid composition—a flesh-technology-information amalgam;
- Relies on machines to make and record discrete observations.

In this respect, a common problem [Ref16] with surveillance is that once monitoring systems have been implemented in one domain, their alleged effectiveness is often used as a reason to adopt the same or similar solutions in other domains [Ref17]. New strategies for control in the form of surveillance infrastructures are continuously developed and novel uses of already existing surveillance networks are extended. Once surveillance regimes have been implemented these systems are seldom modified to be less invasive or withdrawn altogether—unless in conflict with the existing legal framework or met with (exceptional) public outrage. To the contrary, their range and scope is often extended [Ref18].

4.2.1 *Impact of AI surveillance technologies on the values of privacy, autonomy and trust*

From an ethics point of view, the use of AI systems and associated surveillance technologies and additionally the information gathered by them is particularly sensitive with regard to the values of privacy, trust and autonomy that they may affect. Privacy is a boundary concept, which rests on the conception that autonomous individuals enjoy a sphere within which they can conduct their private affairs separate from the public sphere of the government [Ref19]. Linked closed to the issue of privacy is that of trust: privacy is often held in an inverse relationship to trust such that the more trust exists between two people, the less need there is for privacy [Ref20]. Surveillance therefor diminishes the need to trust the person under surveillance.

The concept of privacy can be subdivided into a series of boundaries [Ref21]:

- spatial boundaries that see privacy "activated" when a space such as the home is viewed by an agent of government or unauthorised citizen;
- behavioural boundaries identify activities that are meant to be secured from unwanted attention, such as sexual behaviours or medical matters or other "intimate" activities including those of the mind;
- Informational boundaries can identify kinds of information that are deserving differing levels of protection, such as information pertaining to one's sexuality, religion, and increasingly between the content of communications versus the metadata associated with that content.

Ethical concepts of privacy boundaries support the data protection and information privacy laws, which are themselves meant to "allow individuals rights to control their information and impose obligations to treat that information appropriately" [Ref22].

4.2.2 *Moral risks associated with AI surveillance technologies*

Privacy is at the centre of the moral risk of intrusion associated with AI surveillance technology; we could identify three "moral risks" in relation to the three distinct categories of harm of detection technologies: intrusion, error and damage to trust [Ref23].

- ***The moral risk of intrusion*** involves penetration of one of three distinct 'zones' of privacy: bodily privacy, privacy of home spaces, and private life (penetrated by inappropriate scrutiny of associational life and matters of conscience). An important factor is whether information uncovered by the initial intrusion is made available to further people, as intrusion is usually made worse by sharing information. In this respect, technologies that delete information upon initial use, or do not store information for further viewing preserve the privacy of those under surveillance.

- ***The moral risk of error*** could derive from a number of sources: (1) if the information acquired by the technology is susceptible to false positives this will contribute to errors: some information targeted by surveillance technologies is inherently ambiguous and potentially misleading; (2) technology itself producing/generating, or revealing information which may be highly error prone: data mining technologies often involve profiling algorithms that are susceptible to false positives; (3) some technologies require extensive training and may be vulnerable to errors because of mistakes by the user or viewer; (4) storage may lead to repeated risks of error as well, either because of risks of data corruption, or simply because a later viewer does not have all the information to put the intelligence stored in its proper context. It is not the error in itself that represents a moral problem, but only if the error leads to a sanction of the person under surveillance, such as intrusive searches or arrests.
- ***The moral risk of damage to valuable relations of trust*** refers to two categories of social trust eroded by uses of technology. The first category is the trust in policing authorities that may be damaged by what is perceived as excessive, ethically problematic uses of technology. The second category is interpersonal social trust among the population – damage to this social trust is sometimes referred to as the 'chilling effect' [Ref24]. The damage to both of these kinds of trust result from the perception of at least four morally problematic possibilities on the part of the general public: (1) the perception of the intrusiveness of the technology; (2) the perception of error resulting from the technology; (3) the perception that the technology poses risks of discrimination – either that the technology is disproportionately likely to be used against particular groups or, even, that application of the technology may be more likely to cast suspicion on particular groups, as is the case for example with data mining technologies which make use of crude profiling techniques; (4) the perception of function creep [Ref25] also contributes to this damage to social trust.

4.2.3 *Principles of ethical use of surveillance technologies*

Most discussions of the ethics of surveillance are informed by the Principles of Fair Information Practice that forms the basis of the OECD Guidelines and most national legislation. These were first laid out in 1998 in a Federal Trade Commission (FTC) report "Fair Information Practice Principles" [Ref26], which has been retired, but the underlying messages within the principles remain apparent in more up-to-date directives including the General Data Protection Regulation (GDPR) and OECD Privacy Guidelines originally published in 1980 but updated in 2013 [Ref27]. This model include: 1) accountability 2) identifying purposes 3) openness 4) limiting collection 5) limiting use, disclosure and retention 6) accuracy 7) safeguards 8) individual access 9) compliance.

4.2.4 *Institutional governance for AI surveillance technologies*

AI surveillance technologies, by their nature, are associated with a very high degree of uncertainty about their future deployment and thus a correspondingly broad range of ethical and societal issues are likely to emerge.

It is important that LEAs implement policies for addressing ethical issues systematically, and that they have a governance system implemented at institutional level. Governance is the system of administration and supervision through which research is managed, participants and staff are protected, and accountability is assured [Ref28].

This section presents some relevant points for Law Enforcement Agencies (LEAs) to consider when defining a system of governance for AI systems and associated technologies [Ref29]. Many LEAs already have policies and procedures in place to address a variety of ethical and legal issues that arise in an operational context. It is therefore important that new policies and procedures are only created to complement the existing ones, based on new risks likely to arise from the use of AI surveillance technologies. In that vein, the following guidelines are presented:

- Create a governance system by combining policy guidelines and soft law (i.e. quasi-legal instruments) with hard law. Soft law (such as codes of conducts, guidelines) is usually non-binding and is also a flexible tool that could be easily modified and adapted to changing circumstances.
- Establish a functional accountability of ethical process and designate a point of functional accountability for this responsibility (e.g. Institutional Ethics Board, Ethics Officer).
- Promote ethical, societal and fundamental rights impact assessments of the tools based on an operational setting.
- Promote and sustain fundamental rights "by design and by default" approach (value sensitive design) for the deployment and use of the AI surveillance technologies
- Deploy the technologies that demonstrate enhanced security and diminished negative ethical, fundamental rights and other societal implications – compared with other possible technological solutions or available technologies.
- Comply with the adequate regulation, control and licensing regime to prevent the AI surveillance technologies being "misused" outside a given jurisdiction, and contrary to established fundamental rights and ethical standards.
- Educate and raise awareness among law enforcement professionals regarding the ethical issues of using AI surveillance technologies. We hope that this handbook could assist the LEAs in this endeavour.
- Seek advice from external experts, because properly addressing ethical concerns requires a depth of knowledge that cannot realistically be expected from decision-makers and operational planners.

4.3 AI systems for law enforcement: ethical issues and governance measures

In the last 20 years, due of the rise of transnational organised crime and global terrorism, there are new approaches to safeguard national and personal security. As a result of the spatial and temporal unpredictability of criminal actions and of their global repercussions, a safer society is often pursued through the implementation of policies foreseeing the adoption and deployment of surveillance technologies based on AI systems [Ref30]. Surveillance functionalities are embedded in the design of AI technologies to allow constant monitoring, prevention and investigation. However, as presented before, surveillance technologies bring along with their implementation ethical risks [Ref31], such as risks of privacy infringement, discrimination, misuse, abuse, or errors, which have often triggered public resistance. The same measures meant to foster human security can potentially make people feel insecure, vulnerable, and exposed (chilling effect, function creep).

There are four major categories of AI surveillance technologies [Ref32]

- Public space surveillance: smart CCTV;
- Network and targeted device surveillance (cyber-surveillance): Deep packet inspection for Internet surveillance, content surveillance on targeted devices, location tracking;
- Biometrics: face recognition;
- Data matching, linkage & analysis: including big data, data mining, and visualisation of results).

Taking into consideration the fact that the use of these AI surveillance technologies provides inherent privacy and other ethical issues, we present for each technology, governance measures that could be implemented at institutional level to maintain lawfulness and ethical deployment.

4.3.1 *Public space surveillance: smart CCTV*

CCTV (Closed Circuit Television) is among the most common surveillance technologies to serve a large array of security objectives from detection to deterrence and enforcement [Ref33]. It is used to monitor objects or subjects and is extensively used in many domains in public and private spaces such as national borders, airports, train stations, shopping malls, public transport and urban environments. CCTV plays a significant role in the post-incident investigation of serious crime and CCTV footage is a major investigative tool [Ref34]. Smart CCTV is a more comprehensive surveillance tool, involving advanced features of the technology such as face & motion detection, crowd & directional flow detection, unattended or missing object detection, facial recognition, license plate recognition, targeting/positioning/tracking of subjects and objects, behavioural pattern and anomaly recognition, image quality and camera zooming enhancement, audio recording, and additional data matching and analytics capabilities[Ref35]. The technology is not fully effective as it is difficult to implement prerequisites for camera positioning, lighting and other conditions to produce adequate image qualities. Also, Smart CCTV has impact on human rights in regards to principles of proportionality and discrimination, as the enabling algorithms depend on stereotypical pre-definition of what is to be considered "normal" and "abnormal"[Ref36].

Potential governance measures

It is important to conduct a Data Protection Impact Assessment (DPIA) at an early stage of implementation and deployment to eliminate or reduce the ethical and legal risk [Ref37]. Moreover, it is advisable to consult a data protection authority during a process of prior checking before implementing new CCTV systems.

Other potential governance measures are listed below [Ref38]:

- Exclusion of sensitive areas, e. g. windows with a view into private property, by obfuscating, masking etc. or limiting the zooming-in functionality;
- Limitation of camera record to only relevant events (e. g. left luggage);
- Excluding or limiting audio surveillance;
- De-identification of individuals which are not of interest (pixelating, blurring, blackening, obfuscating, masking);
- Limiting the time frame of surveillance measure deployment;
- Encrypted storage media;
- Access controls regarding video records and reversibly excluded parts;
- Access logging;
- Appropriate data breach notification process;
- Automated deletion routines aligned with specified time periods (legal deletion deadline at the latest);
- Documentation of privacy and security analysis of the full Smart CCTV System and deployed measures for evaluation;
- Transparency on whether and in which scope the camera is recording data, and information on the responsible data controller;
- Regular privacy and security audits of all components including the analytics algorithms.

4.3.2 *Network and targeted device surveillance (cyber surveillance)*

Cyber-surveillance [Ref39] (e.g. Data- Analysis/Filtering & Screening, Deep Packet Inspection (DPI), Data-Mining, surveillance of web 2.0 and social media, etc) describes modalities for monitoring and observing "persons, objects or processes that is based on new technologies and that is operated from and on data networks, such as the Internet" [Ref40]. Cyber surveillance affects human rights in multiple respects: (1) affects the privacy of personal data, of personal communication: (2) has impact on freedom of expression, the trustworthiness of communication and other core values in democratic societies. Prominent use of cyber-surveillance in a European context are Deep Packet Inspection and Location Tracking Technologies.

Deep Packet Inspection (DPI)

DPI is a technology which can be used to extract user data sent between different devices via networks. DPI is a label for a collection of applications that detect and shape live traffic on a network. They recognise patterns in and across TCP/IP packets, the data format standardised for transmitting information over the Internet. The primary technical capability here is the ability to recognise: DPI has been developed to detect applications, protocols, media content, viruses or any other data in a specific format. Recognition then supports two further capabilities: manipulation and notification; manipulation is the ability to act on the detection, by blocking, prioritising or de-prioritising, or otherwise regulate the flow of certain traffic; notification concerns actions around the extracted, such as generating reports, alarms or billing incidents [Ref41].

DPI can be seen as the most all-embracing method of data packet inspection, leading to a comprehensive surveillance of data transmissions between devices. This technology is able to analyse headers as well as payloads of each layer of the packet. Thus, this technology is well equipped to learn the content of the communication between two users [Ref42].

DPI technology has high potential to be misused for social discrimination, political repression, censorship and serious infringement on sensitive areas of private life [Ref43]. Authoritarian governments and political regimes already employ DPI as a means for censorship and control of public communication (e.g. Syria, China, Iran).

Location Tracking Technologies

Modern mobile communication has led to a significant expansion of technologies providing a variety of location systems [Ref44]. Location Tracking Geo-Data, GPS and Mobile Tracking allow tracking of the movement and location of both people and objects. Its most common uses are in the domains of rescuing people, tracking valuable objects or locating criminal suspects. Within a security context, these capabilities enable the concerned authorities to locate, track and possibly identify persons and assets which potentially pose a threat to public security. The repeatedly collected or requested location data, even in anonymised or pseudonymised form, may reveal information about frequently visited places, enable predictions about future whereabouts, determination of means of transportation (by foot, car etc., how fast is the person moving?), allow an assessment of likely living or work places, and last but not least make the identification of the individual possible.

Potential Governance Measures

Potential limitations of DPI in relation with privacy risk mitigation are mainly governance measures e.g., limiting the depth, breadth and data retention, and ways to notify users [Ref45]. Regarding location tracking technologies, the governance measures in this field will mostly entail restricting access to data bases. At least, it is possible to strive for improved IT security of the systems themselves to counter weaknesses of the respective technologies and their settings (e.g. in the GSM networks) as well as to prevent unauthorised access by unauthorised third parties.

4.3.3 *Biometrics: facial recognition*

Biometrics refers to automated methods of recognising individuals based on measurement of their physical or behavioural characteristics [Ref46]. The primary biometrics based on physical characteristics currently include ocular recognition (that is, retina and iris), facial recognition, fingerprints/palm prints, hand geometry, and vein pattern recognition. A biometric system is basically an automated pattern recognition system that either makes identification or verifies an identity by establishing the probability that a specific physiological or behavioural characteristic is valid. The field of application of biometric technologies is wide and ranges from access control in security areas to border and migration control or different kinds of profiling activities. Their main objective is the identification of individuals, whether criminal offenders, undocumented migrants, terrorists, or other suspects.

Facial recognition is one of the biometric techniques already being used in a multitude of areas and still subject to intensive research with regard to further fields of application [Ref47]. Due to weaknesses of two-dimensional (2D) facial recognition systems, research & development efforts of the last years have concentrated on the development of three-dimensional (3D) recognition processes taking into account the three-dimensional condition of the human face, but still the results are highly dependent on the type of deployed technology and the quality of enrolment, templating and matching processes. Depending on the system pre-configuration and algorithms used, the facial physiognomy allows for conclusions regarding age, gender, ethnic origin or even health status of the person. The last two traits especially belong to the category of sensitive personal data, whose processing may occur only under specific legal preconditions. Also, the collection of ethnicity data in particular triggers some risk potential regarding racial discrimination issues. Moreover, the creation of unalterable and unique digital biometric reference sets make them ideal connectors or linking points for any kind of profiling, making it even more important to process and store the personal data securely and within legal limitations.

Potential Governance Measures

For facial recognition, a number of Privacy by Design approaches have been endorsed by experts, and research is still seeking to find and improve means of preventing unauthorised secondary uses, loss, or misuse. Some core factors to enhance privacy in biometrics were data minimisation, maximum individual control, and improved security. The retention of biometric images shall be limited to minimise the potential for unauthorised secondary uses, loss, or misuse. Function creep should be avoided and adequate methods for authentication, communication and data security should be established. In the context of these data security enhancing measures, templates stored in data bases should be encrypted sufficiently [Ref48]. Further possible governance measures [Ref49] are:

- General enhancement of IT security as protection against data theft;
- Protection against infiltration of foreign/inaccurate data, e. g. via electronic signatures of the reference templates;
- Recognition of characteristics copies (anti-spoofing measure);

- Safeguarding the authenticity of the enrolment data, e. g. by supervision of staff present;
- Logging of relevant processes and transactions

4.3.4 Big data, data matching, linkage and analysis

Big data is a common denomination for extremely large data sets that may be analysed computationally to reveal patterns, trends, and associations, especially relating to human behaviour and interactions. Big Data entails a number of different elements [Ref50], such as:

- The degree of complexity within the data set;
- The amount of value that can be derived from innovative vs non-innovative analysis techniques;
- Longitudinal information supplements the analysis.

A 2011 McKinsey report explicitly mentions promising techniques deemed suitable to serve the purpose of Big Data. According to the report, these include data fusion and integration, association, rule learning, classification, cluster analysis, crowdsourcing, ensemble learning, genetic algorithms, machine learning, natural language processing, neural networks, predictive modelling, regression, sentiment analysis, signal processing, supervised and unsupervised learning, simulation, time series analysis, pattern recognition and anomaly detection, and ultimately, the visualisation of results [Ref51].

In terms of ethical risks, there is a very real danger of so-called function creep by extensive profiling. Privacy issues are inherent because sometimes the data collected and analysed may reveal more than was desired, the principle of "purpose limitation" is strongly violated, and contextual integrity cannot be kept.

Profiling and Data Linkage

Profiling [Ref52] is the process of collecting and analysing data on people's individual characteristics, personal information, or activities by either monitoring their actions or other surveillance technologies that can be interfaced with a database. It refers to all those sets of statistical and mathematical data mining techniques applied to datasets containing information about people's choices, preferences and characteristics (this mostly includes data merging from different data sources into larger databases). Part of profiling activities is clustering people into groups that respond to specific criteria, such as the extent to which their behaviour may be considered risky or dangerous. Based on analysing data structure and properties, profiling allows identification of certain individuals or groups. Behavioural profiling addresses potential and actual threats, and has serious privacy implications especially in terms of privacy of personal behaviour.

Reinforced screening and monitoring activities of flight passengers for aviation and border control is highly prioritised on the EU security agenda, such as by processing Passenger Name Records (PNR) and the Advanced Passenger Information System (APIS) which can also contain biometrical data. These approaches mainly affect privacy of personal behaviour, privacy of personal data and, potentially, privacy of personal communication. Besides the primary aims for flight and border security, collected data are also used for law enforcement (e.g. to combat terrorism and crime but also for immigration control) and are exchanged between different national authorities. Partly they rely on the active cooperation of travelling customers as some measures are optional for passengers to accelerate security checks.

Exceptional prudence is required when conducting profiling of behaviour using pattern based network analysis [Ref53] especially where the inferences drawn are then utilised to extrapolate ensuing behaviour via a predictive approach.

Indiscriminate use, and reliance upon the application of data mining techniques to data collated from network sites result in the monitoring of a broad range of persons not suspected of any wrongdoing. When combined with other factors influencing the motives for profiling activities, some of these people will be further subject to intrusive surveillance merely on the basis of the profiling itself, again without any suspicion of wrongdoing on their part. It is very important in this context that the search terms be specific, otherwise broader "profiles that reflect unexamined generalisations" will be reflected, and as such would not respect the principle of proportionality.

Potential Governance Measures

There are six key recommendations for responsible and sustainable deployment of big data (in accordance with GDPR) [Ref54]:

- anonymise personal data, where personal data is not necessary for the analysis;
- be transparent about the use of personal data for big data analytics;
- embed a data protection impact assessment process into big data projects to help identify privacy risks and address them;
- adopt a privacy by design approach in the development and application of big data analytics;
- develop ethical principles to help reinforce key data protection principles;
- Implement internal and external audits of machine learning algorithms to check for bias, discrimination and errors.

5. Ethical Impact Assessment of AI systems for law enforcement

This section articulates the framework for the ethical risk assessment for AI systems and associated AI surveillance technologies when deployed by law enforcement. The information should be used for training of law enforcement users and for raising awareness and making possible the translation of the ethical and legal framework to an operational and practical guideline.

5.1 Methodology

Ethical Impact Assessment (EIA) is defined as a process during which an organisation, together with stakeholders, considers the ethical issues or impacts posed by a new project, technology, service, program, legislation or other initiative intended to identify risks and solutions. As a tool to assess the ethical impact of an emerging technology, EIA was introduced in 2010/2011 as a structured meta-methodology to complement the already established Privacy Impact Assessment (PIA) [Ref55].

One of the first EIA frameworks, which also included PIA, was proposed by Wright in 2011. The framework is structured on the four principles posited by Beauchamp and Childress [Ref56] (respect for autonomy, non-maleficence, beneficence and justice) together with a separate section on privacy and data protection. The author identifies key social values and ethical issues that are drawn from the European Convention of Human Rights (ECHR) and provides some brief explanatory contextual information, which is then followed by a set of questions aimed at the technology developer or policy-maker to facilitate consideration of ethical issues. In addition, the framework includes a set of ethical tools and procedural practices that can be employed as part of the ethical impact assessment [Ref57].

In Table 1 (overleaf) we provide an overview of the different approaches for ethical impact assessment [Ref58] comparing them according to their main focuses, approaches for gathering data for the EIA, stakeholder participation and the main innovation each approach brings to the field.

Table 1. Approaches to Ethical Impact Assessment

Approach	Focus	Data Gathering	Participation	Main innovation
Ethical Technology Assessment	Identify adverse effects of technologies at an early stage.	Checklist assessment by stakeholders	Stakeholders	Identification of ethical issues at an early stage.
Techno-ethical Scenarios	"Soft" impacts of R&I.	Scenario building	Stakeholders	Identification of ethical issues in use-scenarios.
	Ethical issues of emerging Information and communication technologies.	Text analysis of government and research community	Ethicists, policy makers	Structured identification and analysis of ethical issues.
Ethical Impact Assessment	Giving ethics assessors the tools to conduct an ethical impact assessment.	Surveys, workshops, checklists, ethics matrix	Experts and stakeholders	Providing a comprehensive toolkit for assessors.
Anticipatory Technology Ethics	Identifying ethical issues of emerging technologies in the design phase.	Checklist of ethical issues applied to different stages of technology development	Ethicists	A theoretical framework to deal with different levels of ethical analysis. Also adds a robust foresight approach.
Human Rights Impacts Assessment	Measuring the effects of R&I on human rights.	Analysis of records and regulations	Policy makers, stakeholders	A framework that is based on the well-established convention of human rights.
Model for the Ethical Evaluation of Social Technical Arrangements	Engage stakeholders in the ethics assessment process.	Stakeholder engagement meetings	Ethicists, stakeholders	A dynamic theoretical framework that guides stakeholder engagement.

In this respect, the impact assessment framework that we propose introduces two new ethical tools that combine the **Ethical Impact Assessment** and **Techno Ethical Scenario** approaches aimed at the phases of deployment and use of AI systems for law enforcement:

- **Ethical Risk Assessment Form** [Ref 59] **(ERA Form) (Appendix 1)**: This Form provides an opportunity to explore the extent to which the AI system and tools challenge the established ethical values, principles and legislations. Electronic versions of these forms and example assessments are available from CBRNE Ltd. https://www.cbrneltd.com/contact_us.html
- **Misuse Risk Assessment Form (MRA Form) (Appendix 2)**: This Form provides an opportunity to engage in anticipatory risk assessment in respect of the possibility for the misuse of AI systems for law enforcement. Electronic versions of these forms and example assessments are available from CBRNE Ltd. https://www.cbrneltd.com/contact_us.html

For both ethical impact assessment tools we have chosen a methodology based on risk assessment, as it allows for an integrated cycle. This comprises the identification, assessment, and prioritisation of ethical risks followed by the coordinated and efficient use of resources to monitor, minimise, and control the probability and/or impact of the risks occurring [Ref60]. Both impact assessment tools use the same fundamental model Ethical Risk Calculation System (ERCS), which is that the Ethical Risk (ER) can be calculated from an assessment of the Probability (P) of an event occurring and the severity (S) of the consequences if it does occur. The model used is that ER= P * S; the results are for guidance and for further discussion only.

The value of the ERA and MRA Forms lie in their ability to direct the attention of LEA end-users to those aspects with the greatest ethical impact. They also reveal ways of reducing that impact, assuring general compliance with ethical recommendations and legal requirements. The tools are intended to be used during the deployment and use phase, as they underline specific risks related to the governance institutional framework that needs to be implemented by LEAs.

The process for using the two tools is shown in Figure 1 overleaf.

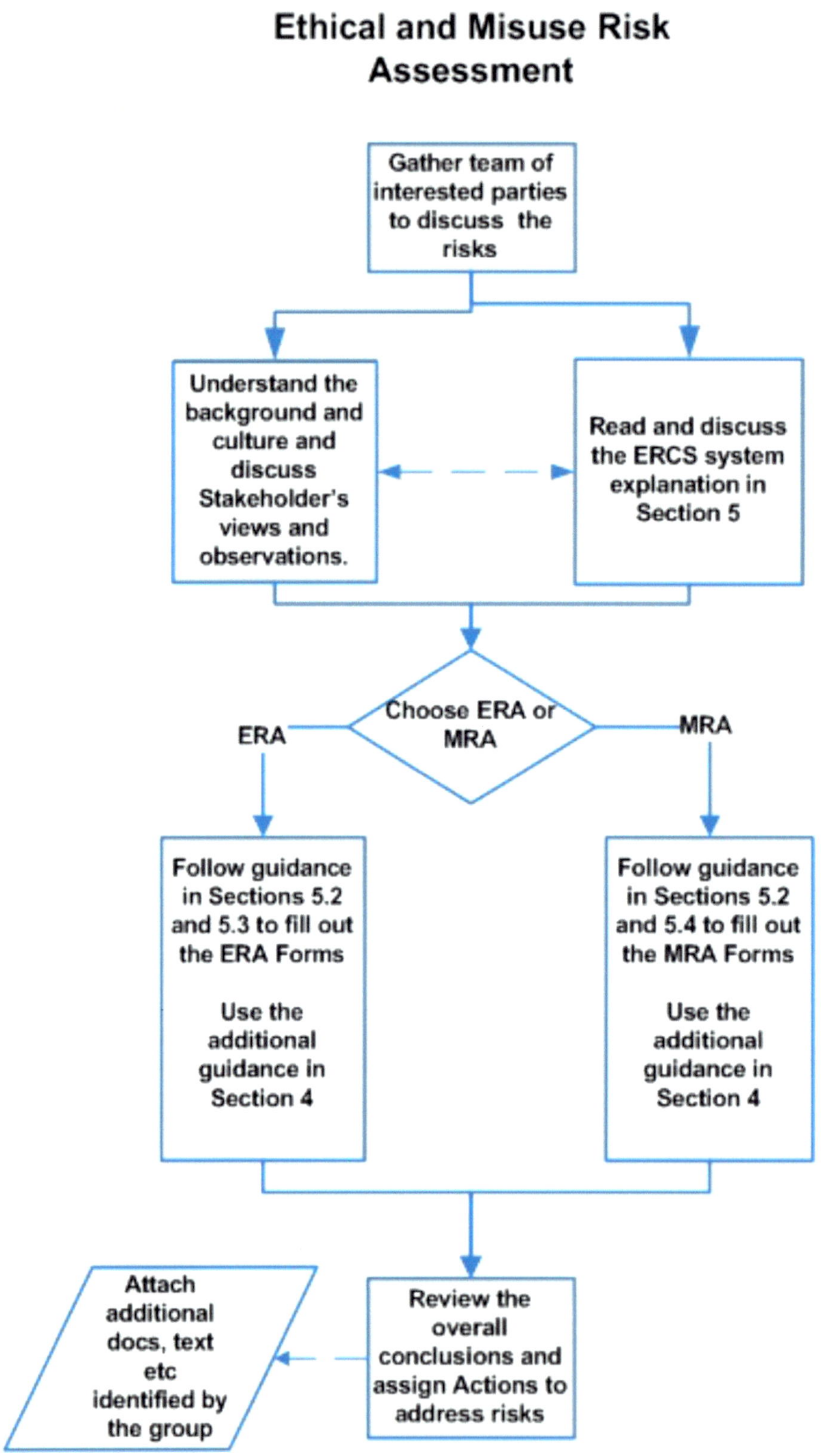

Figure 1: ERA and MRA Process

Considering the potential legal issues raised by the use of AI systems in law enforcement, the ethical risk assessment process presented in this handbook should complement the Data Protection Impact Assessment (DPIA), which is a legal obligation under data protection law. DPIA consists of an assessment of the likelihood and severity of the risks of processing operations likely to result in a high risk to the rights and freedoms of natural persons [Ref61. The GDPR requires controllers to carry out a DPIA to evaluate, amongst others, the origin, nature, detail and severity of the risks. By completing a DPIA, the law enforcement agencies will be able to conduct a deep analysis of the processing activities expected to be performed in an AI system. This will result in the identification of the privacy, data protection and other legal concerns, as well as the ethical issues arising from the technology. Further, this exercise will foster the participation of the different stakeholders. The joint efforts of the stakeholder participants in the DPIA process will result in the proposal of technical and operational measures to mitigate the identified concerns. This DPIA will not only help the law enforcement agencies to comply with the data protection requirements, but will also assist end-users when complying with the DPIA requirement under the DPLED.

5.2 How to use Ethical Risk Classification System

The ethical and misuse risk assessment is based on the following two factors:

- **Severity:** this is the impact of the identified issue. The ERCS provides for this to be Negligible, Marginal or Critical as shown in Table 2.
- **Probability:** This represents the likelihood or chance that the issue will cause the challenge when deployed. The ERCS provides for this to be Low, Medium or High as shown in Table 2. The probability may be expressed 'per deployment' or per year (for example), so the likely frequency of deployment should be considered. Ensure the basis of the assessment is recorded in the assessments.
- **The overall Risk** is shown in Table 2 for each combination of Severity and Probability.
- High risks should be considered to be unacceptable under any circumstances. Medium risks are possibly acceptable but require additional justification. Low risks are likely to be acceptable if you are sure all reasonable measures have been taken to address them. Note these categories are for guidance only and in all cases impacts should be reduced as far as is reasonable practicable.

The ECRS is built into an electronic version of both the ERA and MRA Forms available from info@cbrneltd.com. It does the calculations for you but you can also enter the risks manually into the tables in Appendices 1 and 2.

Table 2: Risk matrix for ERCS

		Severity		
		Negligible Not likely to have a major effect	**Marginal** Has an effect on the action(s) but will not affect the outcome(s)	**Critical** Will affect the action(s) and will affect in a negative way the outcome(s)
Probability	**Low** This risk will hardly occur	Low (1)	Low (3)	Medium (5)
	Medium This risk will likely occur	Low (2)	Medium (6)	High (8)
	High: This risk will occur and has occurred in the past	Medium (4)	High (7)	High (9)

5.3 Ethical Risk Assessment Tool and Form

The Ethical Risk Assessment (ERA) Tool and Form assists law enforcement users in considering and mitigating the ethical risks associated with deployment and use of AI surveillance technologies. The Form part of the Tool is shown in Appendix 1.

5.3.1 *Ethical Risk Assessment framework*

The ERA framework of ethical values and principles draws from the Ethics Guidelines for Trustworthy AI document proposed by the EU Independent High-Level Expert Group on Artificial Intelligence (HLEG) [Ref62] and adapted to the particularities of AI surveillance technologies.

According to the Guidelines, trustworthy AI should be:

- lawful - respecting all applicable laws and regulations
- ethical - respecting ethical principles and values
- robust - both from a technical perspective while taking into account its social environment

Based on fundamental rights and ethical principles (*respect for human autonomy, prevention of harm, fairness and explicability)*, the Guidelines put forward a set of 7 key requirements that AI systems should meet in order to be deemed trustworthy.

1. **Human agency and oversight**: AI systems should empower human beings, allowing them to make informed decisions and fostering their fundamental rights. At the same time, proper oversight mechanisms need to be ensured, which can be achieved

through human-in-the-loop, human-on-the-loop, and human-in-command approaches

2. **Technical Robustness and safety**: AI systems need to be resilient and secure. They need to be safe, ensuring a fall-back plan in case something goes wrong, as well as being accurate, reliable and reproducible. That is the only way to ensure unintentional harm can be minimised and prevented.
3. **Privacy and data governance**: besides ensuring full respect for privacy and data protection, adequate data governance mechanisms must also be ensured, taking into account the quality and integrity of the data, and ensuring legitimised access to data.
4. **Transparency**: the data, system and AI business models should be transparent. Traceability mechanisms can help achieving this. Moreover, AI systems and their decisions should be explained in a manner adapted to the stakeholder concerned. Humans need to be aware that they are interacting with an AI system, and must be informed of the system's capabilities and limitations.
5. **Diversity, non-discrimination and fairness:** Unfair bias must be avoided, as it could have multiple negative implications, from the marginalisation of vulnerable groups to the generation of prejudice and discrimination. Fostering diversity, AI systems should be accessible to all, regardless of any disability, and involve relevant stakeholders throughout their entire life circle.
6. **Societal and environmental well-being**: AI systems should benefit all human beings, including future generations. It must hence be ensured they are sustainable and environmentally friendly. Moreover, they should consider the environment, including other living beings, and their social and societal impact should be carefully considered.
7. **Accountability**: Mechanisms should be put in place to ensure responsibility and accountability for AI systems and their outcomes. Auditability, which enables the assessment of algorithms, data and design processes plays a key role therein, especially in critical applications. Moreover, adequate and accessible redress should be ensured.

5.3.2 *How to use the ERA Tool and Form*

1. LEA decision makers should use the Form as part of the ethics and legal governance processes of the tool. It is important to identify the context of use (law enforcement environment or counterterrorism) and/or specific use case/scenario.
2. The user should select from the requirements presented in the Form or add their own: examples are included with the Form in Appendix 1. The table in the form should be expanded to include further challenges, as required.
3. Using the ERCS table in Section 5.2 select the relevant Initial Risk Level and record this in the Form – if you are using the electronic version just click in the initial risk cell and the ERCS table will pop up for you to select the risk.
4. Identify the 'Controls' - these are the mechanisms in place to mitigate the risk. Examples of Controls are (a) privacy and data protection by design and by default, (b) compliance with legislation & regulations, (c) the inclusion of advice on the issue in the training of the users, (d) reference to the process of ethical governance, etc.

5. Calculate the residual risk using the ERCS table in section 5.2 - the 'Residual risk' is the level of risk that remains, based on a reasonable assessment of the effectiveness of the specified controls. For example, training can be forgotten under stress and therefore it cannot fully mitigate a risk. However, if a particular ethical issue is of little concern locally, the initial risk will already be "Low" and training might suffice to reduce it to As Low As Reasonably Practicable (ALARP).
6. Actions should be specified in the Form to reduce the risk to ALARP, whatever the level of residual risk. Evidence of the resolution of the Actions should be appended to the Form.
7. The results of the Ethical Risk Assessment should be discussed by the development team and/or decision makers.
8. The completed Forms should be retained for the record and for review.

5.4 Misuse risk assessment Tool and Form

The Misuse Risk Assessment Tool and Form assist law enforcement users in considering and mitigating the ethical risks that could rise from the misuse of AI surveillance technologies. The Form part of the tool is shown in Appendix 2.

5.4.1 Misuse risk assessment framework

To identify the potential misuse of AI surveillance technologies, we have relied on the analysis of the 3 moral risks related with surveillance technologies, as identified in section 4.2.2: the moral risk of privacy intrusion, the moral risk of error, and the moral risk of damage to relations of trust.

In respect to the misuse of AI surveillance technologies, we have identified 4 main categories of potential risk, each with specific challenges, as shown in the Table 3.

Table 1: The risks of misuse of AI surveillance technologies and specific challenges

Moral risk	Misuse risk	Specific challenges
Moral risk of privacy intrusion	The LEA user does not comply with the legal framework relevant to the activity.	Improper ethical and legal governance.
		Lack of transparency and accountability.
The moral risk of error	Possibility of error in using the tool leading to an infringement of human rights.	Lack of training
	Surveillance results could fall into wrong hands by error.	Improper security and cybersecurity measures.
		Improper governance of collection, sharing, storage and archiving of surveillance results.
		Unlawful use of tool by LEAs for mass surveillance purposes.

Moral risk	Misuse risk	Specific challenges
The moral risks of damage to relations of trust	The tool is used by the LEAs in an improper way leading to an infringement of human rights	Mission / function creep leading to unauthorised / inappropriate use.
		Possibility of malevolent use of the tool by a LEA employee for personal reasons.

5.4.2 *How to use the MRA Tool and Form*

1. LEA decision makers should use the Form as part of the ethics and legal governance processes of the AI surveillance technologies. It is important to define an operational scenario (law enforcement, counterterrorism, etc.) to identify a specific misuse risk: the ethical challenges will differ according to the context or situation.
2. The user should select from the Misuse Risks presented in the Form (Appendix 2) or add their own. The table in the Form should be expanded to include further challenges, as required.
3. Using the ERCS table in Section 5.2 select the relevant Initial Risk Level and record this – if you are using the electronic version just click in the initial risk cell and the ERCS table will pop up for you to select the risk.
4. Identify the 'Controls' - these are the mechanisms in place to mitigate the risk. Examples of Controls are (a) privacy and data protection by design and by default, (b) compliance with legislation & regulations, (c) the inclusion of advice on the issue in the training of the users, (d) reference to the process of ethical governance, etc.
5. Calculate the residual risk using the ERCA table in section 5.2 - the 'Residual risk' is the level of risk that remains, based on a reasonable assessment of the effectiveness of the specified Controls. For example, training can be forgotten under stress and therefore it cannot fully mitigate a risk. However, if a particular ethical issue is of little concern locally, the initial risk will already be "Low" and training might suffice to reduce it to As Low As Reasonably Practicable (ALARP).
6. Actions should be specified in the Template to reduce the risk to ALARP, whatever the level of residual risk. Evidence of the resolution of the Actions should be appended to the Template.
7. The results of the Misuse Risk Assessment should be discussed by the development team and/or decision makers.
8. The completed Forms should be retained for the record and for review.

6. Conclusion

This Handbook introduces and describes the ethical issues inherent in the use of AI systems in law enforcement.

The discussion of the fundamentals of the subject of ethics leads on to the strong inter-relationship between ethics, society and law – which is illustrated by the volume of Human Rights legislation at national and international level.

The ERA and MRA Forms help to direct attention of law enforcement users to those aspects with the greatest ethical impact and to illuminate ways of reducing that impact, so as to assure general compliance with ethical recommendations and legal requirements.

The information in this Handbook should be of value to law enforcement professionals when considering the development of policy and strategy regarding AI surveillance technologies, as well as in planning and operational stages.

7. References

1 This requires the definition of common standards for security-related equipment as well as the establishment of EU-wide certification schemes for new security technologies. With regard to the standard, the Commission recently mandated European standardization organisations to produce a "privacy by design" standard. As stated by the Commission «compliance with this standard will ensure that EU security products and services respect individuals' rights and thereby enhance consumer confidence». Commission, *Communication Security Industrial Policy Action Plan for an Innovative and Competitive Security Industry,* COM(2012) 417 final, Brussels, 26.7.2012, available at http://eur-lex.europa.eu/LexUriServ/LexUriServ.do?uri=COM:2012:0417:FIN:EN:PDF.

2 General Data Protection regulations, available at https://gdpr-info.eu/

3 Directive 2016/680 on the on the protection of natural persons with regard to the processing of personal data by competent authorities for the purposes of the prevention, investigation, detection or prosecution of criminal offences or the execution of criminal penalties, available at https://eur-lex.europa.eu/legal-content/EN/TXT/?uri=celex%3A32016L0680

4 Recommendation CM/Rec(2010)13 of the Committee of Ministers of the Council of Europe on the Protection of Individuals with Regard to Automatic Processing of Personal Data in the Context of Profiling, Adopted on 23 November 2010, available at https://rm.coe.int/16807096c3

5 European Convention of Human Rights, available at https://www.echr.coe.int/Documents/Convention_ENG.pdf ; Charter of Fundamental Rights of the European Union available at https://eur-lex.europa.eu/legal-content/EN/TXT/?uri=celex%3A12012P%2FTXT

6 European Commission's High-Level Expert Group on Artificial Intelligence. (2019). *Ethics Guidelines for Trustworthy AI* available at https://ec.europa.eu/digital-single-market/en/news/ethics-guidelines-trustworthy-ai

7 MAGNETO – Multimedia Analysis and Correlation Engine for Organised Crime Prevention and Investigation, H2020 786629 project. MAGNETO aims to enhance LEAs capabilities with new data-oriented technologies and solutions. These will permit LEAs to consistently process massive heterogeneous (mixed type) data and find hidden, yet relevant, relationships within it. The system will be learning from user input and adapting the outputs to assist the data analysis through the use of machine learning and augmented intelligence. This will help with the transformation of data into solid and court-proof evidence.

8 Van de Poel I., Royakkers L., Ethics, Technology, and Engineering, Wiley-Blackwell, 2011, p 71

9 Almond, B., 'Applied Ethics', in Craig, E., (ed.), The Shorter Routledge Encyclopaedia of Philosophy, New York: Routledge, 2005

10 Beauchamp, T.L., 'The Nature of Applied Ethics,' in R.G. Frey, ed., *A Companion to Applied Ethics*, Oxford: Blackwell, 2003, p. 12;

11 Reding A., Van Gorp A., Robertson K., Walczak A., Giacomantonio C., Hoorens S., Handling ethical problems in counterterrorism, RAND Europe, 2014, p.7, available at http://www.rand.org/content/dam/rand/pubs/research_reports/RR200/RR251/RAND_RR251.pdf

12 Van de Poel, I. and L. Royakkers, 'The Ethical Cycle,' in Journal of Business Ethics, Vol. 71 No. 1, 2007, pp. 1–13

13 Dworkin, Ronald, *Law's Empire (Legal Theory)*, Belknap Press, 1986;

14 Petersen, J.K. Handbook of surveillance technologies, 3d ed., CRC Press, Taylor & Francis Group (2012) p. 10.

15 Galič, M., Timan, T. & Koops, BJ. Bentham, Deleuze and Beyond: An Overview of Surveillance Theories from the Panopticon to Participation. *Philos. Technol.* **30,** 9–37 (2017). https://doi.org/10.1007/s13347-016-0219-1,

16 Palm, E. 2014. Conditions under which Surveillance may be Ethically Justifiable—Remarks on Kevin Macnish's proposed normative theory of surveillance. *Surveillance & Society* 12(1): 164-170.

17 As noted by David Lyon, surveillance systems originally intended to perform narrowly specified functions are expanded as a reaction to new (political) circumstances, often sidestepping or pushing back the limits of the original legal framework and safeguards in Lyon D., Surveillance Study: an overview, Polity, 2007

18 Practices that before September 11th would have found little acceptance such as biometric identification and authentication processes, dataveillance and large-scale information sharing between countries etc., have been normalised

19 Parsons C, (2015) Beyond Privacy: Articulating the broader harms of pervasive mas-surveillance, in Media and communication 2015, vol 3, issue 3, pp 1-11.

20 Rachels*, J.,* "Why Privacy is Important" *Philosophy and Public Affair*s, 4(4), (Summer, *1975*): 323-333.

21 Parson C (2015), idem, p.4.

22 Parsons, C, Bennett, C J., Molnar, A. (2015), Privacy, surveillance, and the democratic potential of the social web, in Roessler, Beate and Mokrosinska, Dorota (ed), *Social dimensions of privacy : interdisciplinary perspectives*, Cambridge University Press, Cambridge, pp.202-222

23 Deliverable D2.2 Paper with input from end-users (2013) FP7 SEC 2011 284725 Project SURVEILLE: Surveillance: ethical issues, legal limitations and efficiency, available at: https://surveille.eui.eu/wp-content/uploads/sites/19/2015/04/D2.2.Paper-with-Input-from-End-Users.pdf

24 "Chilling effect" is the idea that laws, regulations, or state surveillance can deter people from exercising their freedoms or engaging in legal activities, in Penney J (2017), Internet surveillance, regulations and chilling effects online: a comparative case study, in Internet Policy review, vol.6, issue 2, available at https://policyreview.info/articles/analysis/internet-surveillance-regulation-and-chilling-effects-online-comparative-case

25 "Function creep" is the *gradual widening of the use of a technology or system beyond the purpose for which it was originally intended, especially when this leads to potential invasion of privacy, in Safdar M. and all (2016) Function Creep in surveillance techniques, in International Journal of Scientific Research in Science, Engineering and Technology, vol 2, issue 2, available at* https://www.academia.edu/25501943/Function_Creep_in_Surveillance_Techniques

26 Federal Trade Commission: Privacy online: fair information practices in the electronic market place, available at https://www.ftc.gov/reports/privacy-online-fair-information-practices-electronic-marketplace-federal-trade-commission

27 OECD Privacy Guidelines, available at http://www.oecd.org/internet/ieconomy/privacy-guidelines.htm

28 Show, S., Boyton, P.M., Greenhalgh, T., Research Governance: where did it come from, what does it mean? In Journal pf the Royal Society of Medicine, vol. 98, Nov. 2005, pp 496-502, available at https://www.ncbi.nlm.nih.gov/pmc/articles/PMC1275997/

29 *Apud* Chameau J-L., Ballhaus W., Lin H.S.,(eds) 'Emerging and Readily available Technologies and national security – A framework for addressing Ethical, Legal and Societal Issues', National Academies Press, Washington DC, 2014

30 Perel, M. and Elkin-Koren, N., Ceyhan A, Tsoukala A, the signification of migration in western societies: ambivalent discourses and policies, in Alternatives: global, local, political, vol 27. Issue 1, 2002, pp 21-39

31 Esposti S.D., Gomez E.S., Acceptable surveillance-orientated Security Technologies: Insights from the SurPRISE Project, in Surveillance & Society, vol 13 (3/4): pp 437-454.

32 Deliverable D3.1 Report on surveillance technology and privacy enhancing design, (2013) FP7 SEC 2011 284725: Project SurPRISE: *Surveillance, Privacy and Security: A large scale participatory assessment of criteria and factors determining acceptability and acceptance of security technologies in Europe*, available at: http://surprise-project.eu/dissemination/research-results/

33 D. Litzau (2007). Closed-Circuit Television and Video Surveillance. Information Security Management Handbook, Sixth Edition. H. F. Tipton and M. Krause. Boca Raton, CRC Press: 1349-1356.

34 Clive, N. (2010). Closed-Circuit Television. International Handbook of Criminology. S. G. Shoham, P. Knepper and M. Kett, CRC Press: 395-424

35 Deliverable D3.1 Report on surveillance technology and privacy enhancing design, (2013) FP7 SEC 2011 284725: Project SurPRISE: *Surveillance, Privacy and Security: A large scale participatory assessment of criteria and factors determining acceptability and acceptance of security technologies in Europe*, available at: http://surprise-project.eu/dissemination/research-results/

36 This is for example a weakness of the aforementioned "automatic action recognition" functionality, which predetermines certain actions of individuals and thus is not yet able to ascertain unforeseen activities of individuals, see the article by Adi Robertson, "Military-backed surveillance prototype can read people's actions on video", available at https://www.theverge.com/2012/10/28/3567048/carnegie-mellon-video-surveillance-action-recognition

37 Deliverable D3.1 Report on surveillance technology and privacy enhancing design, (2013) FP7 SEC 2011 284725: Project SurPRISE: *Surveillance, Privacy and Security: A large scale participatory assessment of criteria and factors determining acceptability and acceptance of security technologies in Europe*, available at: http://surprise-project.eu/dissemination/research-results/

38 Deliverable D3.1, Project SurPRISE, op cit, p.14.

39 Cyber surveillance includes network surveillance which is a more technically coined term.

40 Tremblay, M.,(2012): "Cyber-Surveillance", in L. Coté and J.-F. Savard (eds.), Encyclopedic Dictionary of Public Administration [online]

41 Mueller, M. (2011) DPI Technology from the standpoint of Internet governance studies: An introduction, *apud* Asghari, Hadi and van Eeten, Michel and Bauer, Johannes M. and Mueller, Milton, Deep Packet Inspection: Effects of Regulation on Its Deployment by Internet Providers (September 25, 2013). TPRC 41: The 41st Research Conference on Communication, Information and Internet Policy, available at SSRN: https://papers.ssrn.com/sol3/papers.cfm?abstract_id=2242463

42 Deliverable D3.1 Project SurPRISE, op cit, p 29

43 Cf. Ben Wagner, "Deep Packet Inspection and Internet Censorship: International Convergence on an 'Integrated Technology of Control", pp. 2 f.; Christian Fuchs, "Implications of Deep Packet Inspection (DPI) Internet Surveillance for Society", p. 25, apud Deliverable D2.3 Major security challenges, responses and their impact on privacy- selected security orientated surveillance technologies, (2013) FP7 SEC 2011 284725: Project SurPRISE: *Surveillance, Privacy and Security: A large scale participatory assessment of criteria and factors determining acceptability and acceptance of security technologies in Europe*, available at: http://surprise-project.eu/dissemination/research-results/

44 Deliverable D2.3 Major security challenges, responses and their impact on privacy- selected security orientated surveillance technologies, (2013) FP7 SEC 2011 284725: Project SurPRISE: *Surveillance, Privacy and Security: A large scale participatory assessment of criteria and factors determining acceptability and acceptance of security technologies in Europe*, available at: http://surprise-project.eu/dissemination/research-results/, p.38

45 Cooper, A., "Doing the DPI Dance: Assessing the Privacy Impact of Deep Packet Inspection", in: William Aspray, Philip Doty (Eds.), Privacy in America: Interdisciplinary Perspectives, 2011, p. 160.

46 Michelle Chibba, Director of Policy and Special Projects at the Information and Privacy Commissioner's Office in Ontario, Canada, proposals mentioned in her presentation "Biometric Encryption: A Privacy by Design Example for Achieving Citizen Trust" held at the final workshop themed "CryptoBiometrics for Enhanced Trusted ID Management: Dreams & Reality" conducted by the research project TURBINE January 2011 apud D 3.1 Project SurPRISE, op cit p. 61.

47 ibidem

48 ibidem

49 D 3.1 Project SurPRISE, op cit p. 62.

50 Big Data Definition website entry of MIKE2.0, the open source standard for Information Management, http://mike2.openmethodology.org/wiki/Big_Data_Definition

51 James Manyika, Michael Chui, Brad Brown, Jacques Bughin, Richard Dobbs, Charles Roxburgh, Angela Hung Byers, McKinsey Global Institute Report, "Big data: The next frontier for innovation, competition, and productivity", published May 2011 and avail

52 Deliverable 2.3 Project SurPRISE, op cit p.37

53 D4.2 Paper on legal issues related to the use of surveillance data for profiling (2013) FP7 SEC 2011 284725 Project SURVEILLE: Surveillance: ethical issues, legal limitations and efficiency, available at: https://surveille.eui.eu/wp-content/uploads/sites/19/2015/04/D2.2.Paper-with-Input-from-End-Users.pdf

54 Information Commissioner's Office (ICO) Big data, artificial intelligence, machine learning and data protection, version 2.2, 2017, pp 97-98, available at https://ico.org.uk/media/for-organisations/documents/2013559/big-data-ai-ml-and-data-protection.pdf

55 Harris, I., Jennings, R. C., Pullinger, D., Rogerson, S. and Duquenoy, P. (2011) 'Assessment of new technologies: A meta-methodology', Journal of Information, Communication and Ethics in Society, 9: 49–64

56 Beauchamp, T. L., & Childress, J. F. (2009). Principles of biomedical ethics 6th ed. New York: Oxford University Press.

57 Wright, David, (2011) "A framework for the ethical impact assessment of information technology, in Ethics and Information Technology, 13: 199–226, DOI: 10.1007/s10676-010-9242-6

58 Reijers W. & all, (2016) D 4.1 A common framework for ethical impact assessment, FP7 Project SATORI no 612231, Annex A pp.62-63 available at http://satoriproject.eu/media/D4.1_Annex_1_EIA_Proposal.pdf,

59 First version of ERA form was created for Project SUBCOP – Suicide Bomber Counteraction and Prevention, FP7 312375 project. FP7 Security topic SEC-2012-1.3-1 – Less than lethal handling of PBIEDs, see Stănciugelu I, Usher D., Kelly D, (2016) Ethical challenges in the research and development of less than lethal technology, CBRNE available at http://www.cbrneltd.com/Ethical-challenges-in-the-development-of-Less-than-Lethal-Technology.html

60 Francis R.D. (2016) Ethical Risk Management. In: Farazmand A. (eds) Global Encyclopedia of Public Administration, Public Policy, and Governance. Springer, Cham

61 Marquenie, T. Quezada Tavarez, Royer, S. Marsh, I. Kelly, D. (2019) D9.3 Interim Ethical and Legal Assessment, H2020 project MAGNETO

62 EU Independent High-Level Expert Group on Artificial Intelligence (2019) Ethics Guidelines for Trustworthy AI, available at https://ec.europa.eu/digital-single-market/en/news/ethics-guidelines-trustworthy-ai

8. Appendix 1: Ethical Risk Assessment Forms

Ethics Risk Assessment Template		
Name		
Position		
Tool/system		
Date		
Please circle the stage to which the risk assessment refers:		
Research & development (R&D)	Deployment Law enforcement paradigm	Deployment Counterterrorism
Contributors		
Scenario/use-case/discussion		

Ethics requirements		Challenge	Initial Risk (High, Medium, Low)	Control	Residual risk (High, Medium, Low)	Action
Human agency and oversight	Fundamental rights	*- The tool has a negative impact on human rights* *- The tool is affecting human autonomy by interfering with end-user decision making in a unintended way* *- The tool doesn't communicate that a decision/advice or outcome is the result of an algorithmic decision*				
	Human agency	*- The task allocation between the tool and human does not allow for appropriate human oversight and control* *- There are no safeguards to prevent overconfidence /over-reliance in the results offered by the tool*				
	Human oversights	*- There are no mechanisms and measures to ensure human control/oversight (very important if the system is self-learning or autonomous)* *- There are no measures to enable audit in order to remedy identified issues*				

Ethics requirements		Challenge	Initial Risk (High, Medium, Low)	Control	Residual risk (High, Medium, Low)	Action
Technical robustness and safety	Resilience to attack and security	*- There are no mechanisms and measures in place to ensure the integrity and resilience of the tool against potential cyberattacks* *- There are no measures and mechanisms in place to prevent dual-use/misuse*				
	Fall-back and general safety	*- There is not a fall-back plan for adversarial attacks or unexpected situations* *- There are no measures in place to assess risks and safety* *- There is no insurance policy in place to deal with potential damages resulting from the use of the tool* *- There are no measures and mechanism in place to consider the liability due to potential damage or harm to third parties* *- There are no governance measures in place to trigger alternative/fall-back plans*				

Ethics requirements		Challenge	Initial Risk (High, Medium, Low)	Control	Residual risk (High, Medium, Low)	Action
	Accuracy	*- There is no assessment of what harm would be caused if the tool makes inaccurate predictions* *- There are no mechanisms and measures in place to ensure that the data is comprehensive and up to date* *- There are no mechanisms and measures in place to assess if there is a need for additional data in order to improve accuracy or eliminate bias*				
	Reliability and reproducibility	*- There are no verification methods to measure and ensure different aspects of the tool reliability and reproducibility* *- There are no governance systems in place to assure the processes for testing and verification of reliability*				
Privacy and data governance	Respect for privacy and data protection	*- There are no mechanisms for notice and control over personal data depending on the use case* *- The DPO is not involved in the process*				

Ethics requirements		Challenge	Initial Risk (High, Medium, Low)	Control	Residual risk (High, Medium, Low)	Action
	Quality and integrity of data	*- The tool is not aligned with relevant standards (ISO, IEEE) for data management and governance* *- There are no oversight mechanisms for data collection, storage, processing and use* *- There are no processes to ensures the quality and integrity of the data*				
	Access to data	*- There is not an oversight mechanism to log when, where, how, by whom and for what purpose data was accessed* *- There are no protocols, procedures in place to ensure data governance*				
Transparency	Traceability	*-There are no measures/ mechanisms to ensure traceability*				

Ethics requirements		Challenge	Initial Risk (High, Medium, Low)	Control	Residual risk (High, Medium, Low)	Action
	Explainability	*- There is no assessment as to what degree the tool decision influences the decision-making process* *- There is no an explanation of why the system took a certain choice resulting in a certain outcome that all users can understand*				
	Communication	*- There are no mechanisms to inform end-users on the reasons and criteria behind the tool outcomes* *- There is no clear communication on characteristics, limitations and potential shortcomings of the tool*				

Ethics requirements		Challenge	Initial Risk (High, Medium, Low)	Control	Residual risk (High, Medium, Low)	Action
Diversity, non-discrimination and fairness	Unfair bias avoidance	*- Does not consider the diversity and representativeness for specific population or problematic use cases* *- There is no strategy or set of procedures to avoid creating or reinforcing unfair bias in the tool (both regarding the use of input data and for algorithm design)* *- There are no processes to test & monitor for potential biases during the development/deployment/use phase of the tool* *- There are no mechanisms to allows the flag issues related to bias, discrimination or poor performance* *- There are no established mechanisms to ensure fairness in the tool*				
	Accessibility and universal design	*- There is no involvement of end-user community during the development phase of the tool* *- There is no assessment whether persons or groups might be disproportionally affected by the use of the tool*				

Ethics requirements		Challenge	Initial Risk (High, Medium, Low)	Control	Residual risk (High, Medium, Low)	Action
	Stakeholder participation	*- There is no mechanism to include participation of different stakeholders in the development of the tool* *- There is no introduction of the tool in the organisation informing how the workers might be impacted*				
Societal and environmental wellbeing	Sustainable and environmentally friendly AI	*- There is no measure to ensure the environmental impact of deployment and use (type of energy) or the environmental impact of the tool life cycle*				
	Social impact	*-There is no measure to ensure that the social impact of the tool are well understood (ex. risk of job loss, de-skilling of the workforce)*				
	Society and democracy	*-There is no assessment of the broader social impact of the tool beyond the individual end-user*				
Accountability	Auditability	*-There are no mechanisms to facilitate the system auditability (ensuring traceability and logging of the tool systems processes and outcomes)*				

Ethics requirements		Challenge	Initial Risk (High, Medium, Low)	Control	Residual risk (High, Medium, Low)	Action
	Minimizing and reporting negative impact	*- There is no risk impact assessment of the tool that takes into account what the impact is on different stakeholders* *- There are no procedures that support the overall accountability and ethics practices* *- There are no processes for third parties or workers to report potential vulnerabilities, risks or biases in the tool*				
	Documenting trade-offs	*- There is no mechanism to identify relevant interests and values implicated by the tool and potential trade-offs between them*				
	Ability to redress	*- There is no adequate set of mechanisms that allow for redress in case of the occurrence of any harm or adverse impact* *- There are no mechanisms in place to provide information to end-users/third parties about opportunities for redress*				

Ethics requirements		Challenge	Initial Risk (High, Medium, Low)	Control	Residual risk (High, Medium, Low)	Action
Respect of legal restriction on development, use and export of surveillance technology						
Provision of training for users						

9. Appendix 2: MRA Forms

Misuse Risk Assessment Template	
Name	
Organization/Position	
Tool/system	
Date	
Mention the operational scenario to which the misuse risk assessment refers:	

Misuse risks		Challenge	Initial Risk (High, Medium, Low)	Control	Residual risk (High, Medium, Low)	Action
Moral risk of privacy intrusion	The LEA user does not comply with the legal framework relevant to the activity.	*-Improper ethical and legal governance.*				
		-Lack of transparency and accountability.				

Misuse risks		Challenge	Initial Risk (High, Medium, Low)	Control	Residual risk (High, Medium, Low)	Action
The moral risk of error	Possibility of error in using the tool leading to an infringement of human rights.	*-Lack of training*				
	Surveillance results could fall into wrong hands by error.	*-Improper security and cybersecurity measures.*				
		-Improper governance of collection, sharing, storage and archiving of surveillance results.				
The moral risks of damage to relations of trust	The tool is used by the LEAs in an improper way leading to an infringement of human rights	*-Unlawful use of tool by LEAs for mass surveillance purposes.*				
		-Mission / function creep leading to unauthorised / inappropriate use.				
		-Possibility of malevolent use of the tool by a LEA employee for personal reasons.				

Made in the USA
Las Vegas, NV
03 November 2026

57424180R00029